Short cocktails
AND SMALL BITES

More than 25 small-serve drink
& canapé pairings for parties

Julia Charles
Photography by Alex Luck

RYLAND PETERS & SMALL
LONDON • NEW YORK

First published in 2019 by
Ryland Peters & Small
20–21 Jockey's Fields
London WC1R 4BW
and
341 E 116th Street
New York, 10029
www.rylandpeters.com

10 9 8 7 6 5 4 3 2 1

ISBN: 978-1-78879-149-6

A CIP record for this book is available from the British Library. US Library of Congress CIP data has been applied for.

Printed in China.

Dedication
For Bridget, my mother.
Olive you x

Senior Designer
Sonya Nathoo

Editor
Miriam Catley

Production Controller
David Hearn

Editorial Director
Julia Charles

Art Director
Leslie Harrington

Publisher
Cindy Richards

Food Stylist
Lorna Brash

Prop Stylist
Luis Peral

Indexer
Vanessa Bird

Acknowledgements
Big love to every friend I've enjoyed a small drink with. Thanks to Leslie, Sonya, Alex, Luis and Lorna for the stunning design and photos, and to Miriam, for her editorial eye.

The publisher wishes to thank HG Stephensons' for the loan of glassware used in some images. Visit www.stephensons.com to see the full product range.

Contents

Introduction

What is a cocktail? Answer: a cocktail is fun! Simple as that. No matter what the occasion, serving a cocktail elevates it. There's always a frisson of excitement and the mood is instantly lifted when a tray of beautifully presented drinks is passed around. Some of the creations on offer in the world's best bars today are extraordinary and works of mixology genius, but for the keen home-bar amateur or party host, fool-proof recipes and stylish simplicity is always the way forward. In this book I have gathered together a collection of my favourite tried-and-tested cocktails – drinks I've made (and enjoyed) time and time again. They all tick three key boxes – they are created from easy-to-source ingredients, can be whipped up in no time with minimal bar skills, and are frankly delicious.

Classic cocktails often comprise of ratios of straight spirits with no mixers. These so-called 'short' drinks were never intended to be served in generous portions. The martini and negroni, for example, are both strong in flavour and high proof so should be sipped and savoured, accompanied by a satisfying bar bite to soften the blow! And this traditional small serve is perfect for modern entertaining too. It combines the undeniable novelty appeal of a cute, down-sized drink, encourages sensible levels of alcohol consumption and keeps the booze budget under control. Alongside these classic short drinks, you'll also find fun mini versions of popular long drinks, such as sangria and gin and tonic. Either served in a single round as an aperitif or in waves for a drinks' reception, all these recipes offer just enough to break the ice and get the party started.

The accompanying bite-size canapés have been carefully developed to match not only the visual theme of the drinks but to perfectly flavour-pair with their key ingredients too, ensuring an exciting, fully rounded taste experience. I've included ideas for every style of entertaining as well as something for each season (plus all the recipes can usefully be adjusted to cater for crowds). I hope you enjoy trying these small but perfectly formed pairings and find your own go-to favourites, as well as something just right for that special occasion. Cheers!

Singapore sling
with cheese and spicy roasted pineapple sticks

This refreshing gin-based cocktail is said to have been invented at Raffles, Singapore, in 1915 so having marked its 100th anniversary it has surely earned the right to be called a classic. I enjoyed a warm sling garnished with charred pineapple at the Sipsmith 'hot gin roof terrace' at the Ham Yard Hotel, London, which led to the idea for this delicious pairing, which is essentially a pimped-up version of the oh-so-retro 70s party snack.

SINGAPORE SLING

45 ml/1½ oz. gin

10 ml/2 teaspoons cherry brandy

5 ml/1 teaspoon Benedictine

5 ml/1 teaspoon Triple Sec

15 ml/1 tablespoon pineapple juice

30 ml/1 oz. freshly squeezed lemon juice

2 dashes of Angostura bitters

ice cubes, to stir and to serve

soda water/club soda, to top up

lemon zests and cocktail cherries, to garnish

2 small hurricane glasses

Makes 2 drinks (each 60 ml/2 oz.)

CHEESE AND SPICY ROASTED PINEAPPLE STICKS

500 g/18 oz. fresh pineapple cubes

3 tablespoons toasted sesame seeds

¼ teaspoon chilli/hot red pepper flakes (finely ground in a mortar with a pestle)

a handful of fresh mint leaves, very finely chopped

250 g/9 oz. mild Cheddar or Monterey Jack (US), cut into 1-cm/½-inch cubes

cocktail picks, to serve

Makes about 25

Short cocktail: Pour all the ingredients into a small jug/pitcher filled with ice and stir gently to mix. Pour into ice-filled serving glasses, top up with a little soda water/club soda and garnish with a lemon zest and a cherry.

Small bite: Preheat the oven to 180°C (350°F) Gas 4. Put the pineapple cubes into a roasting pan and cook in the preheated oven for 35–40 minutes until golden then cover and set aside to cool. Mix the sesame seeds, chilli/hot red pepper flakes and chopped mint in a bowl. Add the pineapple chunks and toss to coat. Thread the pineapple onto cocktail picks with a cube of cheese and serve.

Classic
and crisp

Mini margarita
with spicy salt lime chicken

Something magical happens when you put chilli, lime and salt together. Whet your guests' appetites with these zingy chicken bites served with a down-sized version of a Mexican classic — the Margarita. No need to salt the rim of the glass here as the chilli salt in the marinade for the chicken adds that essential lip-smacking element.

MINI MARGARITA
50 ml/1½ oz. silver tequila
30 ml/⅔ oz. dry orange curaçao
30 ml/⅔ oz. freshly squeezed lime juice
ice cubes, to shake

2 mini margarita coupes

Makes 2 drinks (each 50 ml/1¾ oz.)

SPICY SALT LIME CHICKEN
500 g/18 oz. skinless, boneless chicken thighs
3 tablespoons light olive oil
2 generous pinches of chilli/chile sea salt flakes
finely grated zest and freshly squeezed juice of 2 unwaxed limes
lime wedges, to garnish
non-reactive shallow dish
cocktail picks, to serve

Makes 40

Short cocktail: Pour the tequila, curaçao and lime juice into a cocktail shaker. Add a handful of ice cubes and shake vigorously for 10–15 seconds. Strain into glasses and serve immediately.

Small bite: Cut the chicken into 40 even-size chunks and put it in the non-reactive dish with 1 tablespoon of the olive oil, a pinch of the chilli/chile sea salt flakes and the zest and juice of 1 lime. Let marinate in the fridge for 2 hours. When you are ready to cook, remove the chicken from the marinade. Heat the remaining olive oil in a frying pan/skillet and sauté the chicken over medium heat for about 5 minutes until cooked through, shaking the pan occasionally. Put in a clean dish with the remaining salt and lime zest and juice. Mix and chill for 1 hour before serving on cocktail picks.

Old-fashioned
with devilled quail's eggs

A Bourbon cocktail just has to be enjoyed with a suitably Southern snack. Devilled eggs are a staple in Kentucky and are guaranteed to show up at every party. These quick and easy mini mouthfuls of creamy egg mayo work beautifully with the caramel and black pepper notes found in a well-made Old-Fashioned.

OLD-FASHIONED
2 white sugar cubes
4 dashes of angostura bitters
100 ml/4 oz. bourbon or rye whiskey
ice cubes
orange zest, to garnish

2 small old-fashioned/rocks glasses

Makes 2 drinks (each 50 ml/1¾ oz.)

DEVILLED QUAIL'S EGGS
6 quail's eggs
1 teaspoon mayonnaise
¼ teaspoon Dijon mustard
dash of Tabasco sauce, or to taste
sweet smoked Spanish paprika (pimenton dulce), to garnish
smoked salt flakes

Makes 12

Short cocktail: Put a sugar cube in each rocks glass. Splash with the bitters until the cube is saturated. Muddle until crushed and syrupy, adding just a little water if necessary to achieve this. Pour in the bourbon and add ice. Stir and then twist the orange zest on the surface of the drink just to release the orange oils and drop it into the glass.

Small bite: Rinse the eggs under warm water. Place in a saucepan and cover with cold water. Bring to a boil and cook for 4 minutes. Drain, rinse under cold running water, peel and pat dry. Cut the eggs in half lengthwise. Gently scoop out the yolks with a very small coffee spoon and put them into a bowl. Add the mayonnaise, mustard and Tabasco and mash. Fill the whites with the yolk mixture, dust with paprika, add a pinch of smoked salt flakes and serve.

Negroni
with parmesan bites with tomato pesto and basil

Surely nothing is as quintessentially Italian as a classic Negroni? Serve this addictive combo of vermouth, gin and Campari ice cold as an aperitivo, along with melt-in-the-mouth Parmesan nibbles, topped with a tangy tomato pesto and fragrant fresh basil.

NEGRONI

50 ml/2 oz. Antica Formula sweet vermouth, chilled

50 ml/2 oz. gin, chilled

50 ml/2 oz. Campari, chilled

ice cubes, to serve

orange zests, to garnish

4 small, straight-sided tumblers, chilled

Makes 4 drinks (each 40 ml/1¼ oz.)

PARMESAN BITES

60 g/2 oz. plain/all-purpose flour

a pinch of fine salt

45 g/1½ oz. salted butter, chilled and diced

60 g/2 oz. finely grated Parmesan

TOMATO PESTO AND BASIL

140 g/5 oz. sun-blushed tomatoes

1 small garlic clove

50 g/1¾ oz. toasted pine nuts, plus extra to garnish

45 g/1½ oz. finely grated Parmesan

2 tablespoons extra virgin olive oil

½–1 tablespoon lemon juice

fresh basil leaves, to garnish

a 4-mm/⅙-inch cookie cutter

a baking sheet lined with parchment paper

Makes 25–30

Short cocktail: Pour all the chilled ingredients into a glass/metal jug/pitcher and stir. Pour into ice-cube filled serving glasses and garnish with a twisted orange zest.

Small bite: Put the flour, salt, butter cubes and Parmesan in a mixing bowl. Rub the butter in until it resembles breadcrumbs. Use your hands to work the mixture into a smooth dough. Roll the dough out on a lightly floured surface until it is 4 mm/⅙ inch thick. Use the cutter to stamp out rounds, transferring them to the prepared baking sheet as you work. Put the sheet to the fridge to chill for 30 minutes. Preheat the oven to 180°C (350°F) Gas 4. Bake in the preheated oven for 8–10 minutes until just golden and crisp. Let cool on a wire rack before topping. To make the Tomato Pesto, purée all of the ingredients (except the basil) in a blender and season to taste. Put a teaspoon of pesto on each Parmesan bite, top with pine nuts and a few basil leaves.

Dry martini
with green olive and anchovy tapenade on crostini

Usually reserved as the cocktail's garnish, here we make a meal of the green olive, literally... Blended with anchovies, capers and garlic into a rich Provençal-style paste and spread on crostini, it's the ideal nibble to enjoy as you sip an ice-cold miniature martini.

DRY MARTINI
15 ml/½ oz. dry vermouth (Noilly Prat)
75 ml/3 oz. London dry gin
(such as Beefeater)
cracked ice
2 mini martini glasses

Makes 2 drinks (each 50 ml/1¾ oz.)

CROSTINI
1 thin frozen part-baked baguette
light olive oil, for brushing

GREEN OLIVE AND ANCHOVY TAPENADE
140 g/5 oz. good quality pitted green
olives in Herbes de Provence
(Belazu are good)
2 anchovy fillets (optional)
1 tablespoon capers, rinsed and drained
1 teaspoon lemon juice
1 small garlic clove
2 tablespoons extra-virgin olive oil
finely grated lemon zest, to garnish
freshly ground black pepper

Makes 20 crostini

Short cocktail: Pour the vermouth and gin over cracked ice in a glass or metal mixing jug/pitcher. Stir to make the cocktail very cold. Strain into 2 small cocktail glasses.

Small bite: To make the crostini, preheat the oven to 190°C (375°F) Gas 5. Use a sharp bread knife to slice the frozen baguette as thinly as possible at an angle. Lay the slices out on a baking sheet and brush each one lightly with olive oil using a pastry brush. Turn and repeat. Place in the preheated oven and bake for about 10 minutes, until crisp and golden brown. Wait until they are cool before topping. (These will keep crisp for up to 1 week if stored in an airtight container.)

To make the tapenade, place all the ingredients in a food processor and purée until well combined and a spreadable paste in texture. Use a teaspoon to top each crostini with the tapenade, smooth slightly across the crostini with the back of a spoon, garnish with a pinch of finely grated lemon zest and a grinding of black pepper. Serve at room temperature.

Bloody mary
with avocado smash, chorizo and tomato topped cocktail blinis

Look no further if you need a little shot of something to kick start a brunch party. This iconic hair-of-the-dog cocktail is even more of a curative when served alongside a satisfyingly squidgy baby pancake, topped with creamy avo smash and spicy chorizo.

BLOODY MARY

50 ml/2 oz. vodka

140 ml/5 oz. tomato juice

10 ml/⅓ oz. freshly squeezed lemon juice

3 dashes Worcestershire sauce

3 dashes Tabasco

a large pinch of salt

a large pinch of freshly ground black pepper

ice cubes

lemon twists, to garnish

celery leaves, to garnish (optional)

celery salt, to rim the glasses

4 small tumblers or shot glasses

Makes 4 drinks (each 50 ml/1¾ oz.)

AVOCADO SMASH, CHORIZO AND TOMATO TOPPED COCKTAIL BLINIS

30 cocktail/mini blinis

2 ripe avocados, halved

1 spring onion/scallion, very finely chopped

2 tablespoons freshly squeezed lime juice

10 thin slices smoked, ready-to-eat chorizo (or meat-free alternative)

10 cherry tomatoes, halved

fresh coriander/cilantro leaves, shredded

salt and freshly ground black pepper

Makes 30

Short cocktail: First prepare the glasses. Spread out some celery salt on a small saucer and add a little water to another. Dip the rim of the glass first into the water, then into the salt. Set aside. Shake all the ingredients together in a cocktail shaker filled with ice cubes and strain into a jug/pitcher. Pour into 4 small tumblers, garnish with a lemon twist and a celery leaf (if using).

Small bite: Heat the blinis according to packet directions. Scoop out the avocado flesh into a bowl. Add the spring onion/scallion and lime juice. Season with salt and pepper. Using a fork, mash and whip until light. Top each warm blini with a teaspoonful of avocado smash, top with a slice of chorizo and half a cherry tomato and garnish with a pinch of coriander/cilantro.

Rusty nail
with home-made mini oatcakes with
honey roast salmon flakes and ginger butter

This blend of Drambuie (a honeyed, herbed and spiced whiskey liqueur) and Scotch was huge in the 60s. Enjoy it today with flakes of moist salmon on crumbly oatcakes, spread with a warming ginger butter. Substitute Bourbon for Scotch and you get a Rusty Spike!

RUSTY NAIL
90 ml/3 oz. Scotch whiskey
90 ml/3 oz. Drambuie
4 small tumblers/rocks glasses

Makes 4 drinks (each 45 ml/1½ oz.)

HONEY ROAST SALMON FLAKES AND GINGER BUTTER
100 g/3½ oz. butter, softened
20 g/¾ oz. fresh ginger, finely grated
140 g/5 oz. hot smoked honey roast salmon flakes (preferably Scottish)
scissored chives, to garnish
freshly ground black pepper

OATCAKES
125 g/4½ oz. wholemeal/whole-wheat flour
150 g/5½ oz. oatmeal, plus extra for dusting
150 g/5½ oz. rolled/old-fashioned oats
1½ teaspoons baking powder
1 teaspoon salt
1 tablespoon soft brown sugar
125 g/4½ oz. butter, melted
4-cm/1½-inch round cookie cutter
baking sheet lined with parchment paper

Makes 20

Short cocktail: Divide the whiskey and Drambuie between 4 ice-filled glasses and stir.

Small bite: To make the oatcakes, preheat the oven to 160°C (325°F) Gas 3. Combine all the dry ingredients in a bowl. Pour in the melted butter and mix. And 3 tablespoons water, a little at a time, kneading into a firm dough. Halve the dough and roll out each piece on an oatmeal-dusted surface to a 3-mm/⅛-inch thickness. Use the cutter to stamp out 20 rounds and place on the prepared baking sheet. Bake in the preheated oven for 15 minutes. Let cool on a wire rack.

For the honey roast salmon topping, beat the softened butter with the ginger. Spread a little butter on each cooled oatcake and top with a few pieces of flaked salmon. Top with a sprinkle of chives and a grinding of black pepper and serve.

Rose and pomegranate cosmo
with pitta chips, eggplant caviar, mint and pomegranate

Petals and pomegranate seeds, an exotic feast for the eyes as well as the tastebuds!

ROSE AND POMEGRANATE COSMO
35 ml/1¼ oz. vodka
20 ml/⅔ oz. triple sec
20 ml/⅔ oz. freshly squeezed lemon juice
25 ml/1 oz. pomegranate juice
1 teaspoon agave nectar
½ teaspoon rose water
ice cubes, to shake
fresh rose petals, to garnish
2 fridge-frosted mini martini glasses

Makes 2 drinks (each 50 ml/1¾ oz.)

EGGPLANT CAVIAR
2 medium aubergines/eggplants

1 garlic clove, crushed
freshly squeezed juice of ½ lemon
2 tablespoons extra-virgin olive oil
1 tablespoon thick, Greek-style yogurt
salt and freshly ground black pepper
chopped fresh mint, to garnish
pomegranate seeds, to garnish
sumac, to garnish (optional)

PITTA CHIPS
2 pitta breads
sunflower oil, to grease
a lightly greased baking sheet

Makes 20

Short cocktail: Add all the ingredients to a cocktail shaker filled with ice. Shake until chilled and then strain into chilled mini martini glasses. Garnish with rose petals.

Small bite: To make the pitta chips, preheat the oven to 180°C (350°F) Gas 4. Slice each pitta in half through the centre so it separates into two pieces. Cut both these pieces in half lengthways and then use scissors to snip each of these 4 pieces into 8 triangles. Arrange these on the prepared baking sheet, cook in the preheated oven for 10 minutes until crisp, then leave to cool. (Leftovers can be stored in an airtight container for 4–5 days.) For the caviar, prick the aubergine/eggplant several times with a fork. Grill/broil it until the skin is black and blistered and the flesh feels soft. When cool enough to handle, peel off the charred skin. Place in a colander. Use your hands to squeeze out as much moisture as possible from the flesh. Place the flesh, garlic, lemon juice, oil and yogurt in a food processor or blender. Pulse to a smooth purée. And salt and pepper to taste. Let cool completely. Spoon a teaspoonful onto each baked pitta chip, sprinkle with fresh mint and a few pomegranate seeds and a pinch of sumac (if using).

Floral and fragrant

Lavender french 75
with goat's cheese and pink peppercorn balls

The epitome of elegance, a French 75 is the perfect aperitif for almost any occasion. Gin, Champagne, lemon juice and sugar syrup – so simple but so effective. This floral twist adds just a hint of perfume, barely there but enough to transport you to the lavender fields of Provence. The canapé pairing is (of course!) a soft goat's cheese, rolled in pink peppercorns and finished with a juicy grape. I like to think Coco Chanel might have enjoyed this treat whilst sitting on the terrace of her villa in the South of France...

LAVENDER FRENCH 75
50 ml/2 oz. gin
25 ml/1 oz. freshly squeezed lemon juice
20 ml/½ oz. Monin lavender syrup
ice cubes, to shake
well-chilled Champagne or Crémant, to top up
lemon twists, to garnish
4 small flutes, such as sherry glasses

Makes 4 drinks (each about 50 ml/2 oz.)

GOAT'S CHEESE AND PINK PEPPERCORN BALLS
200-g/8-oz. soft goat's cheese log
3 tablespoons crushed pink peppercorns
16 seedless green grapes
16 cocktails picks, to serve

Makes 16

Short cocktail: Pour the gin, lemon juice and lavender syrup into a cocktail shaker filled with ice cubes. Shake until frosted then strain the mixture into a small jug/pitcher and divide between 4 small flutes. Top each one with well-chilled Champagne or Crémant and garnish each with a lemon twist. Serve immediately.

Small bite: Cut the goat's cheese log into 16 pieces and roll these into balls. Roll the balls in the crushed pink peppercorns. Insert a cocktail pick into a grape and add the ball. Keep refrigerated until ready to serve.

Bee's knees
with endive cups with roquefort mousse, pear and candied walnuts

The sweetness of this Prohibition era cocktail has found its match in tangy blue cheese.

BEE'S KNEES
25 ml/1 oz. freshly squeezed lemon juice
20 ml/³⁄₄ oz. honey syrup (see below)
50 ml/2 oz. London dry gin, preferably Beefeater
ice cubes, to shake

HONEY SYRUP
140 g/½ cup runny acacia honey
40 ml/⅙ cup hot water
2 mini coupe or martini glasses

Makes 2 drinks (each 50 ml/2 oz.)

ENDIVE CUPS WITH ROQUEFORT MOUSSE, PEAR AND CANDIED WALNUTS
1 tablespoon butter
60 g/¼ cup white sugar
140 g/1 cup walnut halves
125 g/4½ oz. Roquefort cheese
125 g/4½ oz. cream cheese
salt and freshly ground black pepper
1 large ripe Anjou or Bartlett pear, peeled and finely diced
a little freshly squeezed lemon juice
20 small endive leaves, washed and patted dry

Makes 20

Short cocktail: First make the honey syrup. Combine the honey and hot water in a heatproof bowl and stir until completely mixed. Half-fill a cocktail shaker with ice and add the lemon juice, honey syrup and gin. Shake vigorously for 7 seconds until chilled and strain into a coupe glass. Serve immediately.

Small bite: First make the candied walnuts. Heat a non-stick pan/skillet over medium heat and add the butter, sugar and walnuts. Heat for about 5 minutes, stirring constantly until the sugar and butter have melted and the nuts are toasted and well coated in the mixture. Tip them onto a tray lined with parchment paper and quickly separate. Leave to cool. Beat the Roquefort and the cream cheese together until blended and whipped. Season to taste with salt and pepper. Peel and finely dice the pear. Squeeze a little lemon juice over the dice.

To assemble, spoon blue cheese mousse into each endive cup, add a few pieces of diced pear and top with a caramelized walnut.

Chelsea sidecar
with smoked salmon mousse croustades

Replace Cognac in a Sidecar with gin, and this is what you get! A joy I discovered when out of tonic at home but with triple sec to hand. The citrus cuts through the rich salmon.

CHELSEA SIDECAR
45 ml/1½ oz. dry gin
30 ml/1 oz. triple sec
30 ml/1 oz. freshly squeezed lemon juice
1 teaspoon sugar syrup
ice cubes, to shake
lemon twist, to garnish
2 small martini glasses

Makes 2 drinks (each 50 ml/2 oz.)

SMOKED SALMON MOUSSE
100 g/3½ oz. smoked salmon
freshly squeezed juice of 1 lemon
freshly ground black pepper
150 ml/⅔ cup double/heavy cream
4 slices mild smoked salmon, cut into strips
finely chopped dill, to garnish

CROUSTADES
5 large slices of medium-thickness sliced white bread, crusts cut off
2 tablespoons light olive oil
5 cm/2-inch round cookie cutter
24-hole mini muffin pan

Makes 20

Short cocktail: Shake all the ingredients in an ice-filled shaker and strain into a small chilled martini glass. Garnish with a lemon twist.

Light bite: First make the croustades. Preheat the oven to 180°C (350°F) Gas 4. Using a rolling pin, press down heavily onto each slice of bread in turn to roll it out thinly. Brush each flattened slice with oil. Use the cutter to stamp out about 4 rounds per slice. Push each round in the holes of the muffin pan. Bake in the preheated oven for 10 minutes, until lightly coloured and crisp. Allow to cool on a wire rack before filling.

To make the smoked salmon mousse, put the salmon in a food processor with the lemon juice and season with freshly ground black pepper and blitz until the salmon is finely chopped. Add the cream and blitz again until you have a smooth mousse. Store in the fridge until you are ready to serve. To assemble, spoon the mousse into each croustade, top with a piece of smoked salmon. Sprinkle with dill and serve.

Vanilla white lady
with parsnip and apple remoulade
and bayonne ham on rye

Parsnips and apples both flavour pair beautifully with vanilla so a simple French-style remoulade works a treat with this scented twist on the classic White Lady gin and cointreau cocktail. The Bayonne ham is optional here.

VANILLA WHITE LADY
50 ml/2 oz. gin
15 ml/½ oz. freshly squeezed lemon juice
15 ml/½ oz. Cointreau
½ a vanilla pod/bean
ice cubes, to shake
vanilla sugar, to rim the glasses (optional)
2 small martini glasses or coupes

Makes 2 drinks (each 40 ml/1¼ oz.)

PARSNIP AND APPLE REMOULADE AND BAYONNE HAM ON RYE
2 raw parsnips, peeled and grated
1 Granny Smith, grated

finely grated zest and freshly squeezed juice of 1 lemon
100 ml/scant ⅓ cup crème fraîche or sour cream
2 tablespoons good-quality mayonnaise
1 teaspoon wholegrain or Dijon mustard
sea salt and freshly ground black pepper
4 slices of rye bread/pumpernickel, cut into 4-cm/1½-inch squares
70 g/3 oz. air-dried cured ham, such as Bayonne (optional)
a handful of flat-leaf parsley leaves

Makes about 24

Short cocktail: Rim the glasses with sugar, if using. Place the gin, lemon juice, Cointreau and vanilla pod/bean in a cocktail shaker with a few ice cubes. Shake well until frosted, remove the vanilla pod/bean and pour into the sugar-rimmed serving glasses.

Small bite: Combine the grated parsnips and apple in a large bowl and add the lemon juice and toss. In a separate bowl mix together the lemon zest, crème fraîche, mayonnaise and mustard and stir to combine. Season to taste with salt and pepper. Spoon a little remoulade onto each bread square, top with a small piece of ham (if using) and garnish with a sprinkle of flat-leaf parsley to serve.

Aviation
with pea, asparagus and pecorino filo tartlets

This beautiful violet cocktail dates from the early 1900s. Here science comes into play when flavour pairing it as luckily it shares an unexpected affinity with asparagus. Bingo.

AVIATION
50 ml/2 oz. gin
5 ml/1 teaspoon Luxardo Maraschino
5 ml/1 teaspoon crème de violette
25 ml/1 oz. freshly squeezed lemon juice
ice cubes, to shake
Maraschino cherries (ideally Luxardo), to garnish
2 small coupes

Makes 2 drinks (each 40 ml/1¼ oz.)

PEA, ASPARAGUS AND PECORINO FILO TARTLETS

4 sheets of filo pastry (20-cm/7¾-inches square)
2 tablespoons melted butter
2 tablespoons light olive oil
2 shallots, finely chopped
200 g/7 oz. frozen peas
3 tablespoons dry white wine
sea salt
20–25 baby asparagus tips, steamed, to garnish
Pecorino shavings, to finish (optional)
24-hole mini muffin pan, lightly buttered

Makes 20–25

Short cocktail: Add all the ingredients to a cocktail shaker full of ice. Shake until frosted. Strain into small cocktail glasses and garnish with a single Maraschino cherry.

Small bite: Preheat the oven to 180ºC (350ºF) Gas 4. Lay the filo pastry on a large chopping board. (Cover any unused pastry with a clean kitchen towel.) Working with one pastry sheet at a time, brush it all over with melted butter. Cut the buttered pastry into 5-cm/2-inch squares. Create stacks of pastry squares by laying 4 on top of each other at different angles to create a jagged edge. Gently push each stack into the prepared pan. Repeat until all the filo has been used. Bake in the preheated oven until crisp and golden. Carefully remove from the pan and let cool completely.

Heat the oil in a small saucepan set over low heat. Add the shallots and gently sauté for about 3 minutes, until tender and translucent. Add the peas and the wine to the pan. Cover and cook for 3 minutes, until the peas are tender then tip into a food processor and whizz until smooth. Season to taste and let cool. To assemble the tartlets, spoon in the pea purée, add an asparagus tip and a Pecorino shaving.

Sangria straight-up
with manchego and olive pinchos

This undiluted version of the fruity Spanish punch is served over crushed ice and is designed to be sipped rather than quaffed. Make sure all of your ingredients are well chilled in advance. Enjoy with a 'pinchos' stick of Manchego and pimiento-stuffed olives.

SANGRIA

25 ml/¾ oz. Spanish brandy

1 x 750-ml bottle fruity red wine

45 ml/1½ oz. sugar syrup

45 ml/1½ oz. any orange-flavoured liqueur, such as curaçao/triple sec/ Cointreau/Grand Marnier

freshly squeezed juice of ½ an orange

freshly squeezed juice of ½ a lemon

small orange and lemon half-moons, to garnish

mint sprigs, to garnish (optional)

ice chips or crushed ice, to serve

12 small tumblers

Makes about 12 drinks (each 75 ml/3 oz.)

MANCHEGO AND OLIVE PINCHOS

125 ml/½ cup extra virgin olive oil (preferably Spanish)

8 garlic cloves, peeled

1 small unwaxed orange, quartered and thinly sliced (any seeds removed)

3 sprigs fresh rosemary

sea salt flakes

2 x 200-g/7-oz. wedges young Manchego cheese, cut into triangular shards, about 2-cm/¾-inch at the widest end

about 40 pimiento-stuffed Manzanilla olives

20 cocktail picks, to serve

Makes about 20

Short cocktail: Mix all of the ingredients together in a jug/pitcher. Strain into ice-chip filled serving glasses. Garnish each one with an orange and lemon slice and a sprig of mint (if using) and serve.

Small bite: Put the oil in a small saucepan and add the garlic and orange. Heat over low-medium heat for about 10–12, stirring until the garlic starts to turn golden. Remove from the heat and add the rosemary sprigs. Season with a few pinches of salt flakes and let cool before pouring into a bowl. Add the cheese shards and very gently toss to coat. Cover and chill in the fridge for at least 8 hours. When ready to assemble, remove the cheese from the marinade and drain on paper towels. Thread two olives onto a cocktail pick add a Manchego shard and serve.

Fruity and fresh

Pisco sour
with pink grapefruit ceviche-style shrimp skewers

Not widely served, but delicious, this moreish cocktail relies on Pisco, a grape Brandy made and enjoyed in Peru and Chile (though originally fermented by Spanish settlers there in the 16th century). Ceviche however (a dish of marinated raw fish or seafood) has travelled from it's native Peru and gained popularity all over the world. Here a simple citrus marinade gives cooked shrimp an authentic taste of La Paz with the tangy pink grapefruit and lime juices complimenting the lemony bite of the drink.

PISCO SOUR
50 ml/2 oz. pisco
25 ml/1 oz. freshly squeezed lemon juice
15 ml/½ oz. sugar syrup
15 ml/½ oz. egg white
2 dashes of Angostura bitters
ice cubes, to shake
2 sherry glasses or small wine glasses

Makes 2 drinks (each 50 ml/2 oz.)

PINK GRAPEFRUIT CEVICHE-STYLE SHRIMP
finely grated zest and juice
of 1 pink grapefruit
freshly squeezed juice of 2 limes
4 tablespoons light olive oil
1 fresh red chilli/chile, deseeded and finely chopped
½ teaspoon salt
20 tiger prawns/shrimps, cooked and peeled
1 tablespoon chopped coriander/cilantro
1 spring onion/scallion, finely sliced
cocktail picks, to serve

Makes 20

Short cocktail: Add all the ingredients to a cocktail shaker filled with ice cubes. Shake sharply and strain into the small wine glasses.

Small bite: Put the grapefruit zest and juice, lime juice, oil, chilli/chile and salt in a non-reactive bowl. Add the tiger prawns/shrimp, cover and chill in the fridge for 3 hours. Put the chopped coriander/cilantro and spring onion/scallion in a bowl. Remove the prawns/shrimp from the marinade and toss them in the herb and onion to coat. Thread a prawn/shrimp onto each cocktail pick to serve.

Bramble
with peppered beef, with blackberry sauce and watercress toasts

Blackberries and black pepper, a surprising flavour-match successfully explored here!

BRAMBLE
50 ml/2 oz. gin
25 ml/¾ oz. freshly squeezed lemon juice
10 ml/2 teaspoons sugar syrup
ice cubes, to shake
crushed ice, to serve
15 ml/1 tablespoon Crème de Mûre
(blackberry liqueur)
1 lemon slice and a fresh blackberry,
to garnish
2 small tumblers/rocks glasses

Makes 2 drinks (each 50 ml/2 oz.)

PEPPERED BEEF WITH BLACKBERRY SAUCE AND WATERCRESS TOASTS
1 ciabatta loaf
400 g/14 oz. peppered roast beef slices
1 tablespoon olive oil
a handful of watercress

BLACKBERRY SAUCE
1 tablespoon balsamic vinegar
150 ml/⅔ cup beef or vegetable stock
2 tablespoons redcurrant jelly
1 small garlic clove, crushed
85 g/3 oz. frozen blackberries

Makes about 20

Short cocktail: Add some crushed ice to each of the serving glasses. Shake the gin, lemon juice and sugar syrup in an ice-filled cocktail shaker and strain into the prepared glasses. Drizzle half of the Crème de Mûre over the top of each drink so that it bleeds into the pale mixture. (Do not stir.) Garnish with a lemon slice and a blackberry to serve.

Small bite: Preheat the oven to 200°C (400°F) Gas 6. To make the blackberry sauce, add the vinegar to a pan, pour in the stock and add the redcurrant jelly and garlic. Stir over a high heat to mix then add the blackberries and cook until softened. Mash them with a fork and stir. Set the sauce aside to cool. Cut the ciabatta loaf in half lengthways and toast under a hot grill/broiler for about 10 minutes until lighted toasted. Using a serrated bread knife, cut the bread on a diagonal into 5-cm/2-inch diamonds. Tear the beef into bite-size slices and place a few on each toast. Drizzle with the cooled blackberry sauce. Finish each one with a few sprigs of watercress.

La paloma
with spicy mexican corn and queso fresca quesadilla wedges

Sour, sweet and salty, La Paloma gives the margarita a run for its money in Mexico and is served here with a crisply toasted quesadilla oozing with spicy melted cheese and corn.

LA PALOMA

60 ml/2 oz. Silver tequila

30 ml/1 oz. freshly squeezed pink grapefruit juice

15 ml/½ oz. freshly squeezed lime juice

½ tablespoon agave syrup

ice cubes, to shake

pink grapefruit soda or tonic, to top up

pink sea salt, for rimming the glasses

2 small tumblers

Makes 2 drinks (each 50 ml/2 oz.)

SPICY MEXICAN CORN AND QUESO FRESCA QUESADILLA WEDGES

4 small flour tortillas/sandwich wraps (each 18 cm/7 inches diameter)

75 g/3 oz. Mexican queso fresca or mild feta, crumbled

100 g/4 oz. Gruyère, grated

4 tablespoons canned sweetcorn, drained and rinsed

30 g/1 oz. coriander/cilantro leaves, finely chopped

4–6 spring onions/scallions

1 large green chilli/chile, deseeded and finely chopped

salt and freshly ground pepper

4 tablespoons olive oil, for shallow frying

Makes 24

Short cocktail: First prepare the glasses. Spread out some pink sea salt on a small saucer and add a little water to another. Dip the rim of the glass first into the water, then into the salt. Set aside. Pour the tequila, grapefruit juice, lime juice and agave syrup into an ice-filled cocktail shaker and shake until frosted. Strain into the salt-rimmed glasses to serve.

Small bite: Place 2 of the tortillas on a work surface. Divide the cheeses, sweetcorn, coriander/cilantro, spring onions/scallions and chopped chilli/chile and season well with salt and pepper. Press the remaining tortillas on top to make a sandwich. Heat 2 tablespoons olive oil in a large frying pan/skillet over medium heat. Fry the quesadillas one at a time on both sides until light golden and crisp (use a metal fish slice to press them down while cooking and to turn them over). Cut each one into 12 small wedges and serve warm.

Ouzo sunrise
with watermelon, fennel-marinated feta, olive and fresh mint skewers

Sparkling azure seas, sugar-cube white houses with blue shutters and pink bourganvillea tumbling over every doorway... my kind of paradise. You too can be transported to the Greek Islands with these bite-size summer salads on a stick and an ouzo-based cocktail.

OUZO SUNRISE
45 ml/1½ oz. vodka
10 ml/¼ oz. ouzo
30 ml/1 oz. fresh orange juice
a dash of sugar syrup
ice cubes
20 ml/¾ oz. soda/selzer water
orange zests, to garnish
2 small highball glasses

Makes 2 drinks (each 50 ml/2 oz.)

WATERMELON, FENNEL-MARINATED FETA, OLIVE AND FRESH MINT SKEWERS
1 tablespoon fennel seeds
200 g/7 oz. feta cheese
finely grated zest of 1 lemon
1 tablespoon freshly-squeezed lemon juice
2 tablespoons extra virgin olive oil (preferably Greek)
20 small fresh mint leaves, rinsed and patted dry
20 pitted Kalamata black olives
20 even-sized cubes of fresh watermelon, deseeded
20 cocktail picks, to serve

Makes 20

Short cocktail: Add the vodka, ouzo, orange juice and sugar syrup to a cocktail shaker filled with ice. Shake until chilled, strain into the glasses, top up with soda to taste and garnish with an orange zest.

Small bite: Toast the fennel seeds in a dry frying pan/skillet over low heat until golden. Drain and rinse the feta and cut it into 2-cm (¾-inch) cubes. Put the cooled fennel seeds, lemon zest and juice and oil in a bowl. Add the feta cubes and gently toss to coat. Cover and refrigerate for 4 hours. To assemble, simply thread a mint leaf, an olive, a marinated feta cube and a watermelon cube onto each cocktail pick. Serve chilled.

Moscow mule
with crab with radish, caper and ginger
salsa in cucumber boats

This is a sublimely refreshing summer cocktail, traditionally served in a copper mug that frosts with the icy chill of its contents. Enjoy with a cooling cucumber and crab 'boat'.

MOSCOW MULE

freshly squeezed juice of ½ a lime (about 15 ml/½ oz.)

ice cubes, to shake and to serve

60 ml/2 oz. vodka, well chilled

about 180 ml/6 oz. ginger beer, well chilled

fresh mint sprigs, to garnish

lime wheels, to garnish

6 small copper mugs or tumblers

Makes 6 drinks (each c45 ml/1½ oz.)

CRAB WITH RADISH, CAPER AND GINGER SALSA IN CUCUMBER BOATS

2 long, thin cucumbers

250 g/1 cup white crab meat, ideally fresh

100 g/scant ½ cup fromage frais

100 g/3½ oz. radishes, finely chopped

2 tablespoons small capers, rinsed

1 tablespoon scissored chives

2 tablespoons light olive oil

2 tablespoons ginger wine

salt and freshly ground black pepper

20 cocktail picks or forks, to serve

Makes about 20

Short cocktail: Squeeze the lime juice into an ice-filled cocktail shaker. Add the vodka and stir. Pour into mini copper mugs, add an ice cube to each, top up with ginger beer and garnish with a sprig of mint and a lime wheel.

Small bite: For the cucumber boats, peel each cucumber. Cut off the rounded ends and cut it in half lengthways. Use a teaspoon to scrape out the seeds. Slice a thin strip off the bottom of each half to create a flat base. Slice the remaining flesh crossways at 3–4 cm/1¼–1½-inch intervals to create about 20 generous crescents.

Mix the crab meat and fromage frais in a small bowl. Cover and chill. Put the radishes, capers, chives, olive oil and ginger wine in a separate bowl and mix. Season to taste with salt and pepper. To assemble, spoon a little crab mixture into each cucumber boat and top with some of the salsa. Thread a cocktail pick through from side to side or serve with cocktail forks.

Strawberry daiquiri
with strawberry, mango, basil and pine nut salsa on baked tortilla chips

A deliciously fruity rum cocktail and nibble to enjoy poolside on a hot summer's day.

STRAWBERRY DAIQUIRI
4 fresh strawberries, plus extra to garnish
2 teaspoons white sugar
35 ml/1½ oz. white rum
1 tablespoon strawberry liqueur
25 ml/1 oz. freshly squeezed lime juice
ice cubes, to shake
2 mini martini glasses or coupes

Makes 2 drinks (each 40 ml/1¼ oz.)

STRAWBERRY, MANGO, BASIL AND PINE NUT SALSA
100 g/3½ oz. ripe strawberries, hulled and diced
200 g/7 oz. ripe mango flesh, diced
2 tablespoons finely diced red onion
2 tablespoons toasted pine nuts
2 tablespoons chopped basil, plus extra to garnish
1 tablespoon freshly squeezed lime juice
sea salt and freshly ground black pepper

BAKED TORTILLA CHIPS
3 x 15-cm/6-inch flour tortillas
½ tablespoon sunflower oil
sea salt
an oiled baking sheet

Makes 24

Short cocktail: Put the serving glasses in the freezer to frost. Put the strawberries and sugar in a cocktail shaker and mash using a muddler or the end of a wooden rolling pin. Add the rum, strawberry liqueur and lime juice and a few cubes of ice. Shake well until frosted. Strain into the frosted serving glasses to serve.

Small bite: Preheat the oven to 200°C (400°F) Gas 6. Brush the tortillas on one side with oil. Cut each one into 8 even-sized wedges with kitchen scissors. Arrange them oiled-side-up on the prepared baking sheet and sprinkle with salt. Bake for 5–7 minutes until browned and crisp. Let cool on a wire rack.

To make the salsa, put all the ingredients in a bowl and mix. Season to taste. Spoon a little salsa onto each tortilla chip and garnish with a basil leaf to serve.

Apple pie moonshine
with maple-roasted pumpkin
and whipped ricotta bruschetta with sage

I made this fun cocktail for a Halloween gathering with friends (in lieu of actual apple bobbing) but its cinnamon-apple flavours make it perfect for any Fall celebration.

APPLE PIE MOONSHINE

100 ml/4 oz. apple pie moonshine (such as Midnight Moon)

100 ml/4 oz. cloudy apple juice/soft cider

50 ml/2 oz. cinnamon syrup

30 ml/1 oz. freshly squeezed lemon juice

ice cubes, to shake

small green apple wedges, to garnish

cinnamon sticks, to garnish (optional)

4 mini glass tankards

Makes 4 drinks (each 70 ml/2½ oz.)

MAPLE-ROASTED PUMPKIN AND WHIPPED RICOTTA BRUSCHETTA WITH SAGE

3½ tablespoons olive oil, plus extra for brushing the bruschetta

1½ teaspoons maple sugar (or soft brown sugar)

1-lb/450-g butternut squash, peeled, seeded and cut in 1.5 cm/½ inch cubes

1 slim baguette/French stick

24 fresh sage leaves

about 165 g/¾ cup fresh ricotta

½ teaspoon freshly grated lemon zest and freshly squeezed lemon juice, to taste

sea salt and freshly ground black pepper

baking sheet

Makes about 24

Short cocktail: Pour all of the ingredients into an ice-filled cocktail shaker and shake until frosted. Pour into glasses and garnish with an apple wedge and a cinnamon stick.

Small bite: Preheat the oven to 180°C (350°F) Gas 4. Put 2 tablespoons of the oil in a bowl with the maple sugar and add the squash cubes. Toss to coat. Tip out onto a baking sheet in a single layer and roast in the preheated oven for 20–25 minutes, until golden and tender. Preheat the grill/broiler. Thinly slice the baguette on an angle to create long, narrow fingers, drizzle with oil and grill/broil until crispy on both sides. (These toasts can be made a few hours ahead of serving.) Heat the remaining oil in a small skillet over medium/high heat. Add the sage leaves and cook until they curl and are dark green. Use a slotted spoon to remove them from the pan and put on paper towels to drain. Beat the ricotta and lemon zest until light and airy and season with lemon juice, salt and pepper. Spread each bruschetta with ricotta, top with a few cubes of squash and finish with a fried sage leaf.

Festive
and fun

Swedish glögg
with västerbotten and cloudberry jam grilled cheese

Glögg translates as ember and this is the ultimate fireside drink for lovers of anything mulled. It is a party punch and not practical to make in small quantities so this recipe will make about 20 x 75-ml/3-oz. servings, perfect for creating a little 'hygge'.

SWEDISH GLÖGG
peel of 1 small unwaxed orange
1 x 750-ml bottle red wine
375 ml/13 oz. ruby port
250 ml/1 cup brandy
2 tablespoons light brown sugar
1 tablespoon whole cardamom pods, crushed
6 cloves
1 cinnamon stick
small raisins and slivered/sliced almonds, to garnish (optional)
20 small glass tankards

Makes 20 drinks (each 75 ml/3 oz.)

VÄSTERBOTTEN AND CLOUDBERRY JAM/ JELLY GRILLED CHEESE
85 g/3 oz. full-fat cream cheese
10 medium-thickness white bread slices
about 2 tablespoons cloudberry jam/jelly (available from specialist Scandinavian grocers, such as ScandiKitchen)
200 g/7 oz. Västerbotten cheese, or a strong/sharp Cheddar
scissored chives, to finish
cocktail picks, to serve (optional)
a large baking sheet, lined with parchment paper

Makes 20

Short cocktail: Using metal tongs hold the orange peel over a flame on the hob/ cooktop until it spots brown. Drop it into a large pan. Add the wine, port, brandy, sugar and spices. Simmer over medium heat for about 20 minutes then strain into a heatproof jug/pitcher. Pour into small heatproof glasses and add a few raisins and almond slivers to each serving to garnish. Serve with small coffee spoons, if liked.

Small bite: Preheat the oven to 200°C (400°F) Gas 6. Spread the cream cheese onto both sides of each slice of bread. Spread the jam/jelly thinly onto one side of the bread. Sprinkle half the grated cheese over 5 slices of bread. Firmly press the remaining bread slices on top to make sandwiches. Place them on the prepared baking sheet. Sprinkle the remaining cheese across the top of the sandwiches. Bake for about about 10 minutes, until the cheese is golden and melted. Sprinkle with chives, let cool slightly, then cut off the crusts with a serrated knife. Cut each sandwich into 4 small squares and thread 2 of these onto each cocktail pick, if using. Serve warm.

Clementine caipirinha
with brie and cranberry sauce puffs

A classic Caipirinha is my go-to drink on a hot summer's night. It is made with a whole lime cut into wedges and 'muddled' with sugar in a rocks glass to extract all the juice. A scoop of crushed iced then goes in, followed by a generous measure of neat spirit. Rather than be deprived of this icy treat in the winter months, I tried this seasonal twist. The tangy clementine is, of course, perfect with a little cranberry sauce and creamy brie.

CLEMENTINE CAIPIRINHA

1 whole clementine

1 fresh lime, cut into wedges

2 teaspoons demerara sugar

60 ml/2 oz. cachaça (Brazilian sugar cane spirit)

ice cubes and crushed ice

2 small tumblers

drinking straws

Makes 2 drinks (each 30 ml/1 oz.)

BRIE AND CRANBERRY SAUCE PUFFS

375-g/12-oz. package ready-rolled puff pastry, chilled

about 200-g/7 oz. Brie, cut into 2-cm/¾-inch cubes

250 ml/1 cup cranberry sauce

fresh thyme sprigs, to garnish

a 24-hole non-stick mini muffin pan, lightly greased

Makes 24

Short cocktail: Remove the ends from the clementine and slice it into quarters, being sure to remove any of the white pith in the centre of the segments. Put into a cocktail shaker with a lime wedge and sugar and pound with a muddler or end of a wooden rolling pin to extract the juice. Add the cachaça with plenty of ice cubes and shake well. Strain into small crushed-ice filled tumblers and serve with a short, wide straw. Garnish with lime wedges, if desired.

Small bite: Preheat the oven to 200°C (400°F) Gas 6. Use a sharp knife to cut the puff pastry sheet into 7.5-cm/3-inch squares. Press each square into the prepared muffin pan. Place a cube of Brie in each one and add about 2 teaspoons of cranberry sauce. Bake in the preheated oven for 15–10 minutes until golden and puffed and the cheese has melted. Garnish with a sprig of thyme and serve warm.

Espresso martini
with marzipan-stuffed dates with orange blossom water and pistachios

Coffee cocktails are now very much a thing, and so they should be — they are absolutely delicious. Leading the charge is the Espresso Martini — although not a new idea it's only really found mainstream popularity in recent years and is now on every cocktail menu. I am still not convinced it makes a good brunch drink (I prefer something fruity) so save it for after a good dinner when energy levels are flagging and 'second wind' is required. Just a few sips with a sugary petit four ensures hitting the dance floor remains an option!

ESPRESSO MARTINI
50 ml/2 oz. freshly made espresso coffee
50 ml/2 oz. vodka
50 ml/2 oz. coffee liqueur, such as Kalhua or Tia Maria
½ tablespoon sugar syrup
ice cubes, to shake
coffee beans, to garnish (optional)
2 mini martini glasses

Makes 2 drinks (each 75 ml/3 oz.)

MARZIPAN-STUFFED DATES WITH ORANGE BLOSSOM WATER AND PISTACHIOS
24 large Medjool dates
180 g/6 oz. white marzipan
orange blossom water, to taste
finely chopped pistachios, to garnish

Makes 24

Short cocktail: Pour all the ingredients into a cocktail shaker filled with ice and shake until the outside of the shaker feels icy cold. Strain into small martini glasses, garnish with coffee beans (if using) and serve.

Small bite: Make a slit along each date and remove the pits. Knead the marzipan with a few drops of orange blossom water, to taste. Divide the mixture into 24 pieces and gently fill each date with a piece. Finish with a sprinkle of chopped pistachios. These will keep for 2 weeks in an airtight container.

Cinnamon buttered rum
with mini cherry coconut macaroons

Buttered rum just sounds so good doesn't it? The traditional recipe is diluted with water but here it's served neat in a small glass and made with an oak-aged dark rum, flavoured with warming spices, including cinnamon. Both cherry and coconut love a bit of spice so enjoy this hot toddy with a moist and chewy bite-size macaroon on the side.

CINNAMON BUTTERED RUM
25 g/1½ tablespoons butter
2 tablespoons demerera sugar
4 cinnamon sticks
200 ml/1 cup spiced gold rum, such as Captain Morgan's Spiced
2 small glass tankards

Makes 4 drinks (each 50 ml/2 oz.)

MINI CHERRY COCONUT MACAROONS
4 x medium UK/large US egg whites
100 g/½ cup white caster/granulated sugar
1 teaspoon pure vanilla extract
¼ teaspoon fine salt
200 g/3 cups sweetened desiccated/shredded coconut
about 20 undyed (natural colour) glace/candied cherries, very finely chopped
melted dark chocolate, to decorate (optional)
a large baking sheet, lined with baking parchment

Makes about 24

Short cocktail: Gently heat the butter, demerera sugar and cinnamon sticks in a saucepan until the butter has melted and the sugar dissolved. Stir in the rum, transfer to a heatproof jug/pitcher and then pour into heatproof serving glasses. Garnish with a cinnamon stick.

Small bite: Preheat the oven to 175ºC (350ºF) Gas 4. Whisk the egg whites, sugar, vanilla and salt in a large bowl until the mixture is frothy. Add the coconut and chopped cherries and stir until combined. Using wet hands work the mixture into small balls about 3-cm/1¼-inches in diameter. Space them about 2.5 cm/1 inch or so apart on the baking sheet. Bake in the preheated oven for about 10–20 minutes, until golden brown. Let cool on the baking sheet then transfer to a wire rack to cool. Drizzle with melted dark chocolate, if liked, and leave to set before serving.

Snap apple
with beetroot rosti with horseradish cream and dill

The uniquely light and fresh flavours of Scandinavian food come together here. A crisp apple and aquavit shot with a beetroot/beet rosti served with a horseradish cream and aniseedy dill garnish. A whole smorgasbord of fun and flavour in just a few mouthfuls.

SNAP APPLE
ice cubes, to shake
30 ml/1 oz. aquavit
30 ml/1 oz. green (sour) apple liqueur
a squeeze of fresh lime juice
a few dashes of sparkling clear lemonade
green apple slices, to garnish
2 shot glasses

Makes 2 drinks (each 30 ml/1 oz.)

BEETROOT ROSTI WITH HORSERADISH CREAM AND DILL
250 g/9 oz. cooked beetroot/beet, grated

250 g/9 oz. raw potato, grated and squeezed dry
1 tablespoon plain/all-purpose flour
1 egg, beaten
salt and pepper
2 tablespoons sunflower oil
150 ml/5½ oz. sour cream or crème fraiche
1 tablespoon hot horseradish sauce
sea salt and freshly ground black pepper
fresh dill, to garnish
4.5-cm/1¾-inch cookie cutter

Makes 20

Short cocktail: Half-fill a cocktail shaker with ice. Add the aquavit, apple liqueur and a squeeze of lime juice. Shake until frosted then pour into shot glasses. Add an apple slice to each serving and top up with chilled sparkling lemonade. Serve immediately.

Small bite: Mix the grated beetroot/beet, potato, flour and egg together and season well with salt and pepper. Heat 1 tablespoon of the oil in a medium non-stick frying pan/skillet. Spread half the mixture across the base of the frying pan/skillet (about 5 mm/¼ inch thick). Reduce the heat to low and cook for about 10 minutes on both sides, until both sides are crisp and golden. (Use a plate to tip and flip over.) Remove from the pan and cool slightly on kitchen towels. Heat the remaining oil and repeat with the rest of the mixture. Use the cookie cutter to stamp 10 rounds from each rosti cake. Let cool completely. Mix the cream and horseradish together in a small bowl and season to taste. Spoon a little on top of each rosti and garnish with dill. Serve at room temperature rather than cold.

Spiced G&T
with paneer, mango chutney and cashew nut poppadoms

When I eat Indian food it's always with an ice-cold gin and tonic within easy reach — it works so well with the spicy heat. I am also rather partial to poppadoms dunked into mango chutney, hence the idea for using snack-size ones as a canapé base. Topped here with curried paneer cheese, they are the perfect balance of crunch and creaminess.

SPICED G&T

50 ml/2 oz. cardamom-spiced gin, such as Ophir

about 100 ml/4 oz. classic tonic water, well-chilled, to top up

grapefruit zests, to garnish

a few cardamom pods, to garnish

2 mini gin 'copa' or small wine glasses

Makes 2 drinks (each 75 ml/3 oz.)

PANEER, MANGO CHUTNEY AND CASHEW NUT POPPADOMS

1 x 75-g/2½-oz. bag plain mini poppadoms (from the snack aisle in your supermarket)

2 tablespoons mango chutney (remove any large chunks of mango)

1 tablespoon apple cider vinegar

½ teaspoon mild curry powder

2 tablespoons mayonnaise

2 tablespoons plain/natural yogurt

150 g/5¼ oz. paneer (Indian cheese), cut into ½-cm/¼-inch cubes

50 g/2 oz. cashew nuts, roughly chopped

salt and freshly ground black pepper

2 teaspoons dry toasted nigella seeds, to garnish

fresh coriander/cilantro leaves, shredded, to garnish

Makes about 20

Short cocktail: Pour the gin into the glasses and top up with tonic. Stir and garnish with a grapefruit zest and a few cardamom pods.

Small bite: To make the dressing, combine the chutney, vinegar, curry powder, mayonnaise and yogurt and season to taste. Add a few cubes of cheese to each poppadom and top with a teaspoonful of the dressing. Add a sprinkling of chopped cashews, coriander/cilantro and a few nigella seeds to garnish.

Brandy alexander
with salted chocolate-dipped dried figs

Here is a classic rich and creamy cocktail that particularly benefits from being served in a small portion. Add a chocolate-dipped fig dusted with sparkling salt flakes to offset the sweetness and you have an indulgent treat for the legions of salted caramel devotees out there. Serve this pairing as an elegant (and easy to prepare) alternative to eggnog as the grand finale to a festive drinks party.

BRANDY ALEXANDER

60 ml/2 oz. cognac

30 ml/1 oz. dark crème de cacao

30 ml/1 oz. single/light cream

freshly grated nutmeg, to garnish

ice cubes

2 mini martini glasses

Makes 2 drinks (each 60 ml/2 oz.)

SALTED CHOCOLATE-DIPPED DRIED FIGS

100-g/3½-oz. bar 70% cocoa solids dark/bittersweet chocolate, snapped into pieces

12 small semi-soft ready-to-eat dried figs

sea salt flakes

a flat plate or tray lined with parchment paper

Makes 12

Short cocktail: Pour all of the ingredients into an ice-filled cocktail shaker and shake until frosted. Pour into cocktail glasses and garnish with a dusting of freshly grated nutmeg to serve.

Small bite: Melt the chocolate in a heatproof bowl set over a pan of barely simmering water. Ensure that the base of the bowl does not touch the surface. Stir with a rubber spatula until melted. Use your hands to massage the dried figs and shape them into their natural teardrop shape. Dip the base of each one into the melted chocolate and lay it on the tray. Sprinkle sparingly with sea salt flakes and leave to set before serving.

Index

Short cocktails
AND SMALL BITES